BON JOVI
LOST HIGHWAY

ISBN-13: 978-1-4234-4923-2
ISBN-10: 1-4234-4923-1

HAL • LEONARD® CORPORATION

7777 W. BLUEMOUND RD. P.O. BOX 13819 MILWAUKEE, WI 53213

Visit Hal Leonard Online at
www.halleonard.com

LOST HIGHWAY

Words and Music by JON BON JOVI,
RICHIE SAMBORA and JOHN SHANKS

4

(You Want To)
MAKE A MEMORY

Words and Music by JON BON JOVI,
RICHIE SAMBORA and DESMOND CHILD

Ooh, you wan-na make a mem-o - ry?

Repeat and Fade

Optional Ending

SUMMERTIME

Words and Music by JON BON JOVI,
RICHIE SAMBORA and JOHN SHANKS

20

Feels some-thing like sum-mer-time, ___ top down and noth-ing but time. The

ra-di-o's on ___ for me and my ___ val-en - tine. ___

WHOLE LOT OF LEAVIN'

Words and Music by JON BON JOVI
and JOHN SHANKS

It's pret-ty cold _ for late Sep-tem-ber; _

the au-tumn wind _ is creep-ing in. ____

Recorded a half step lower.

rea - son to ___ be strong. ___ Seems ___ like late - ly there's a whole lot of

leav - ing go - ing on.

Close the win - dow, draw the cur - tains, ___

you ain't the on - ly one here _____ hurt - ing.

WE GOT IT GOING ON

Words and Music by JON BON JOVI,
RICHIE SAMBORA, BIG KENNY and JOHN RICH

You got a ___ Oh, ___ oh, ___

hey, yeah, ___ oh. ___

(Spoken:) "And now, a public service announcement from my country cousin."

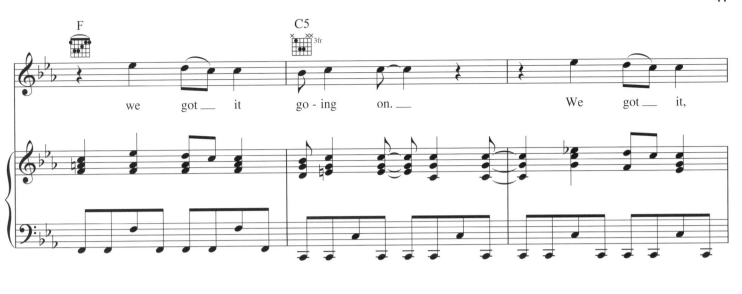

we got __ it go-ing on. __ We got __ it,

we got __ it, we got __ it go - ing on. __

ANY OTHER DAY

Words and Music by JON BON JOVI,
RICHIE SAMBORA and GORDIE SAMPSON

* Recorded a half step higher.

SEAT NEXT TO YOU

Words and Music by JON BON JOVI,
RICHIE SAMBORA and HILLARY LINDSEY

long, slow drive____ down an old dirt road,____ you got your
cor - ner booth of a down - town bar,_____ with your

hand out the win - dow, lis - t'ning to the ra - di - o,____
head on my shoul - der, smok - ing on a cheap____ cig - ar,____

EVERYBODY'S BROKEN

Words and Music by JON BON JOVI
and BILLY FALCON

Moderate groove

Wel-come to the par-ty, ___ come on in ___ and dis-ap- -pear. ___ You're feel-ing like a stran- -ger, but all your friends ___ are here.

to feel a lit - tle bro - ken, ev - 'ry - bod - y's bro -

- ken, you're al - right, it's just life. __

Step in - to the deep end, __

make your - self __ at home. __

62

right,   it's just   life.

TILL WE AIN'T STRANGERS ANYMORE

Words and Music by JON BON JOVI,
RICHIE SAMBORA and BRETT JAMES

THE LAST NIGHT

Words and Music by JON BON JOVI,
RICHIE SAMBORA and JOHN SHANKS

ONE STEP CLOSER

Words and Music by JON BON JOVI,
RICHIE SAMBORA and JOHN SHANKS

Slow Country Rock

I've seen the heart _ of dark — ness,
I hitched a ride with for-give — ness, in that

let's just say I crossed o — ver that line. _____
riv-er of e-mo-tion I went down a third time. _____

Held hands _ with the hope — less, in too deep
I spent the night with the liv - ing, took a chance, _

I LOVE THIS TOWN

Words and Music by JON BON JOVI,
RICHIE SAMBORA and BILLY FALCON

Freely

I al-ways knew _ that I liked _ this place. _

Country Rock

You don't have to look too far ___ to find a friend-ly face. _

___ I feel a-live ___ when I'm